Original title:
Purpose: Still Loading

Copyright © 2025 Creative Arts Management OÜ
All rights reserved.

Author: Kieran Blackwood
ISBN HARDBACK: 978-1-80566-228-0
ISBN PAPERBACK: 978-1-80566-523-6

The Light Behind Closed Doors

In the pantry, cookies hide,
I peek in, barely wide-eyed.
The light flickers, what a scene,
Snack time's here, I'm a snack machine.

Underneath the table's glare,
A cat plots with great fanfare.
What's the mission? What's the plan?
I'm just here to find the Spam!

A Journey Half-Begun

Off I go, half-shod feet,
That shoe's on wrong, how neat!
My map has coffee stains and crumbs,
A compass? No, just jelly drums.

The car's on empty, but who cares?
I'll ride on hopes and sticky prayers.
With snacks piled high and jokes to tell,
Where I'm going? Who can tell?

The Pause Before the Leap

I stand on edge, the world below,
Should I dive or stay in flow?
A bird's eye view, what do I spy?
Just my lunch, if I can fly!

Counting sheep or counting stars,
What is right? Who gives me jars?
With laughter bubbling like a creek,
I'll jump, but first—let's take a tweak!

Finding Meaning in Tides

The waves roll in, a moody beat,
Shells and seaweed at my feet.
I ponder if the fish have dreams,
Perhaps they plot their own grand schemes!

Ebb and flow, a restless dance,
Crabs throw shade; oh, what a chance!
With each splash, I find my glee,
In the chaos, I can see!

A Symphony of Unplayed Notes

Instruments gathered, their hopes in a line,
The conductor's asleep, oh what a sign!
Strings whisper softly, drums snore away,
Melodies waiting for just one more day.

Trombones are slack, flutes lost in a haze,
The triangle jingles, but nobody plays.
A symphony brewing, but oh what a mess,
Instead, it's a concert of awkward silence.

Attuning to the Quiet Pulse

The metronome ticks, but the beat's out of whack,
Singers are yawning, our stage is a snack.
Laughter erupts as we awkwardly sway,
Who knew that a rhythm could lose its way?

We dance with our shadows, a bumbling crew,
Each step is a chance, so what will we do?
A jig or a twist? Perhaps none are right,
As we tread the boards, with our feet full of light.

Dreams on Hold

Post-it notes flutter, ideas in queue,
They cling to the fridge with a hope that is true.
A vision of grandeur, a plan from the past,
But Netflix is calling, so dreams fade at last.

Naps turn to marathons, thoughts drift like foam,
Procrastination's a cozy, familiar home.
"Tomorrow," we whisper, with snacks in hand,
But each passing hour slips right through our sand.

The Rhythm of Hesitation

A leap of intention gets caught in the air,
Deciding which sock goes with which crazy hair.
The clock ticks in beats, but we stop to compare,
Pro and con lists that go nowhere, with flair.

A tap on the shoulder, "Hey, what's the hold?"
We're trapped in a limbo, all hesitant gold.
The dance of indecision grips us with might,
As we stand on the edge of procrastinate fright.

Reflections in a Shimmering Pool

In a pool where dreams collide,
I see my lunch on the inside.
A fish with burger on its plate,
It's late, oh mate, it's way too late!

A frog leaps high with perfect aim,
Splatters me, it's all a game.
The lilies laugh, they float with glee,
While I just crave a cup of tea.

Mirrors gleam, but not a clue,
What's real? Just me and my shoe.
I wave at ducks, they shake their heads,
No answers here, just silly spreads.

So I float, a ship in tea,
With snacks and giggles, just me, just me!
Reflecting on what's yet to be,
In shimmering waves, I find my spree.

The Song of Unclaimed Realities

A cat with wings sings out of tune,
Dancing round beneath the moon.
It claims the stars—what a delight!
    But also steals my pizza bite.

While socks conspire in a drawer,
    Debating who could win a war.
They plan a heist, a daring feat,
To snatch the crumbs I left to eat!

A treasure map leads to the fridge,
But ghosts reside beneath the bridge.
They barter leftovers, chips, and pies,
    While I just roll my weary eyes.

    Somewhere in this chaos bright,
My sandwich dreams ignite the night.
    With laughter spilling, here I roam,
In unclaimed realms, I'm still at home.

Fog and Fireflies

Fog rolled in with a cheeky grin,
Dancing playfully on my skin.
Fireflies waltz with little thrills,
While I look for my missing bills.

They flicker stories, oh so grand,
About a squirrel with a band.
It strummed a tune on a garlic clove,
And made the moon from a studious stove!

With every step, I can't decide,
If I want to run or just glide.
The fog is thick, the paths unclear,
But where's that pizza? Ah, never fear!

So I chase the glow, dart here and there,
While squirrels giggle like they don't care.
In a world of whimsy and twinkling lights,
I find my heart in scattered sights.

Waiting for the Sun to Rise

I sit and stare, the birds still sleep,
While my coffee turns to soup, too deep.
The toaster fights with my last slice,
It's crispy, crunchy, oh so nice!

A shadow moves, I think it's fate,
But it's just my cat, not that great.
She stretches wide, a furry mess,
As I sigh, wish for breakfast bliss.

The clock ticks loud, it plays a tune,
Tick-tock dreams of a sunny June.
But outside, clouds are playing tricks,
Donuts call, they'll do the fix!

So here I am, a morning knight,
Armored in crumbs, with no insight.
But with each giggle, I find the prize,
In every wait, the joy's the rise.

Shadows of Infinite Possibilities

Beneath the bright lights, I stand still,
Searching for answers, what a thrill.
A map in my pocket, with no place to go,
Like a chicken on stilts, I'm still in the show.

Balancing on ideas, they wobble and sway,
Twirling around like it's my birthday.
With every bright thought, a balloon goes pop,
Oh, how I wonder, will I ever stop?

Between the Lines of Existence

I scribble my thoughts on the edge of a napkin,
Chasing down dreams, but they keep on tappin'.
My puns are like magic, they vanish with laughter,
Yet somehow I'm still searching, for what comes after.

In coffee shops, I ponder and frown,
Staring at strangers, can't figure them out.
They say life's a book, but pages are torn,
Maybe I'm just waiting for a unicorn?

The Dance of Doubts and Dreams

A two-step with doubts, a tango with glee,
Life's a great stage, come dance here with me.
Juggling ambitions, with a splash of surprise,
Like clowns in a circus, we all wear disguise.

So I trip on my hopes, but I laugh all the way,
Dreaming of tomorrow, each goofy cliche.
Every slip leads to giggles, each fall makes me cheer,
Oh, to be lost, with no worries, my dear!

Awaits Us in the Silence

In the hush of the night, ideas start to chuckle,
The brain's a playground, ready to shuffle.
Whispers of genius flirt with my ear,
But they run away screaming when I get near!

So I sit in the quiet, and giggle away,
Collecting my thoughts, in a new kind of play.
With each silly notion, I can't help but grin,
What fun to be lost where all journeys begin!

The Space Between Arrivals

In the queue to life's buffet,
Some choices seem to stray.
Life's a playlist on repeat,
Waiting for a brand new beat.

A traffic jam of good ideas,
Where logic disappears.
I trip on socks of yesterday,
Laughing on my clumsy way.

Between the steps, a dance unfolds,
With stories yet untold.
I juggle dreams like rubber balls,
And chuckle as one falls.

Days whizz by like silly kites,
Chasing all the flights.
With every twist and every twirl,
I'm just a kid inside this world.

Pausing at the Crossroads

A giant sign post stands in place,
With arrows in a frantic race.
Left or right, I can't decide,
So I just take a coffee ride.

Guess I'll flip a coin once more,
Heads for there, tails for shore.
It lands on edge, what a twist!
I shrug and laugh, add it to the list.

A chicken walks with such a flair,
Crossing paths without a care.
"Why'd you stop?" I hear it squawk,
"Just out here for a silly talk."

So I sit and sip my drink,
Finding meaning in the blink.
In traffic jams of deep thought,
The chicken's wisdom hits the spot.

Fragments of a Hidden Map

I found a map beneath my bed,
With doodles drawn in red.
X marks the place I ought to be,
But it leads to a lost sock spree.

Treasure hunts in laundry heaps,
Where missing items quietly sleep.
Clues lead to the fridge or yard,
And laughter fails as the task gets hard.

Half the map is drawn in crayon,
The other half just says 'play on.'
Who needs directions in this spree?
Adventure's best with mystery!

Swirling maps in silly dreams,
Finding gems in burst seams.
Every line a giggle's trace,
As I wander this whimsical space.

The Art of Unraveled Intentions

I set my goals in tiny jars,
Each labeled with 'to the stars!'
But every time I open one,
A cloud of dust reveals the fun.

Intentions twist like spaghetti strands,
Finding their way through wandering hands.
I meant to start a serious quest,
But tangled yarn just gives me jest.

Unraveled plans like tumbleweed,
Rolling along, they take the lead.
With every detour that I face,
I end up in a happy place.

So here I am, a jester true,
With every fumble feeling new.
The art of life, a daring prank,
With laughter framing every rank.

The Flicker Before the Flame

A spark ignites, but goes out fast,
The dance of thoughts all tangled and cast.
Chasing dreams like a cat chasing tails,
Sometimes it's fun, sometimes it fails.

With every flicker, a giggle breaks free,
What's cooking up inside? It's hard to see!
Like a firefly lost in a jar,
Just spinning around, oh, how bizarre!

Scraps of a Never-Painted Canvas

Colors splatter, but where is the line?
I'm a kid with crayons, oh, what a design!
Every stroke leads to a chuckle or two,
"Is that a tree or a shoe?" I just don't have a clue.

Mismatched patterns from my mind's big sale,
A masterpiece born from a sloppy trail.
Just when you think you know what it's about,
Turns out it's a trip, not a map, just a shout!

The Unraveling Mystery of Self

Who am I now? Maybe a bit of a clown,
In this circus of life, I balance and frown.
I look in the mirror, and what do I see?
A puzzle that's missing a piece by a bee!

Each day a riddle, like socks in a drawer,
So many options, can't pick just one score.
It's a game of charades, with no end in sight,
I'm just here having fun, come join in the fight!

Roads Taken, Roads Awaited

A fork in the road, oh, which way to turn?
One road is straight, the other has a worm.
With a sigh and a laugh, I choose the fun path,
Who knows what's coming? I'll just take a bath!

With every adventure, a new tale unfolds,
Like socks gone missing, or secrets retold.
I'll skip through the cosmos, just me and my fate,
Creating a story that's worth the long wait!

The Silver Lining of Uncertainty

As I ponder my fate, what a wild ride,
The map's just a doodle, no GPS guide.
I trip on my thoughts, yet I still have glee,
Dancing in circles, like a bumblebee.

With each twist and turn, there's a laugh to be found,
Like a jester on stage, I'm the king of this ground.
Winding through moments, oh, what a delight,
In chaos I find my own glittering light.

So here's to the unknown, my quirky best friend,
A riddle of life that I will never end.
With sidesteps and giggles, I embrace every chance,
For laughter's the compass that leads me to dance.

As I chuckle at fate with a casual grin,
I revel in all that I cannot pin.
The silver lining's here, it's as bright as a star,
Join me, oh world, let's discover who we are!

The Journey of Unwritten Chapters

With blank pages waiting, my pen's in a whirl,
In the theater of life, I'm the lead in this swirl.
I scribble and doodle, plot twists on the way,
Who needs a script when you can play all day?

Each chapter's a riddle, unwritten, absurd,
I ask for a sign, yet no one's heard.
Turning the pages, I tumble and twirl,
Like a cat in a tree, just a drip of a girl.

With coffee and chaos, I'm crafting this tale,
A nonsensical journey on an upside-down rail.
The writing is messy, yet I'm having a blast,
In a world of much humor, I'm free and vast.

So bring on the plot holes, the blunders and quirks,
My story's a circus, with laughter it lurks.
With friends by my side, we'll dance through the gaps,
In chapters unwritten, we'll revel in laps!

In the Space Between Us

In the space between thoughts, there's a giggle or two,
Like socks in the dryer, where'd they go, who knew?
We wander through silence, with quips on the way,
Mixing our laughter like it's gourmet soufflé.

Wi-Fi connections in life, they can be spotty,
But in playful debates, I feel so snotty.
In the chaos of moments, we chase down the fun,
Two odd little peas in a mismatched bun.

Let's fill up the void with puns and some cheer,
As we leap through the air like we're catching a deer.
Giddy with laughter, in the quiet, we bloom,
Cracking up over nothing, you light up the room.

So here's to the space where the weirdos collide,
In this kooky connection, it's a bumpy ride.
With smiles as our glue, we'll stick like some paste,
In the quirky abyss, there's no time to waste!

Awakened Yet Asleep

In the land of the snooze, where dreams come to play,
I'm caught in a spiral of slumber's ballet.
Awakened yet drooping, I'm caught in the blend,
Like butter on toast, both a lover and friend.

Each yawn's a performance, a theatrical act,
I'm practicing naps, but I'm fully distracted.
With pillows for audiences, I sigh and I snore,
In the theater of slumber, I always want more.

Tick-tock goes the clock, but time seems to slide,
As I dance with the dreams, I'm a whimsical ride.
Awakened yet dreaming, in a muddled array,
In a sleepy parade, I frolic and sway.

So here's to the moments that drift through the haze,
In this daisy chain of laughter, I'll spend all my days.
With eyes half-closed, yet a grin ear to ear,
In the space of my dreams, I'm awake with no fear!

The Art of Becoming

I tried to bake a cake, oh what a sight,
Eggs on the ceiling, flour took flight.
It wasn't a dessert, more like a crime,
But hey, it's all part of my grand design.

Dancing in circles, I trip on my feet,
Life's a long sandwich, and I've lost the meat.
Brush strokes of chaos cover my stage,
Creating a masterpiece, one laugh at a time.

In the Limbo of Ambitions

I woke with a dream, a rocket to build,
But I just can't find where I left my drill.
Ambition's a puzzle, where's the last piece?
Guess I'll just roll with this state of unease.

Plans like spaghetti, all stuck on a wall,
I name my pet fish 'The Great Overhaul'.
Each day's an adventure, with snacks on my side,
In limbo of dreams, I'm ready to glide.

A Canvas Yet to Be Painted

With colors in hand, I dive in with glee,
But end up with splatters all over me.
My brush is rebellious, it dances around,
An accidental Picasso? How profound!

The canvas is eager, yet blank and so white,
My thoughts like confetti, in so much delight.
I sketch a big donut, it's round, it's just right,
And laugh at the chaos of artistic flight.

Steps on a Blurry Trail

I set out on pathways, the map's upside down,
But who needs directions in this goofy town?
Each step's an adventure, each turn's a surprise,
I might just find treasure, or meet friendly fries.

The trail's getting fuzzy, like my morning toast,
Fashionably lost is what I love most.
With laughter as fuel, I stumble, I sway,
Life's an odd journey, in the silliest way.

The Weight of Unlived Moments

Socks unmatched, dreams on hold,
Pants that fit, have stories untold.
The couch has become my best fan,
Unraveled plans - oh, where did they land?

I float like a leaf in the breeze,
Dodging chores like I'm on a spree.
The laundry's a mountain, a comedic scene,
I could conquer it all, but my coffee's serene.

A spaghetti dinner, a sitcom plot,
Should I cook? Nah, I think I forgot.
Life strategies drawn on pizza boxes,
I ponder my fate as the microwave boxes.

Balloons full of wishes, they drift and pop,
As I trip on my own feet, butcher a hop.
The weight grows heavy, yet laughter I find,
In every misstep, I leave woes behind.

Moments of Stillness in Motion

Rushing like ants, then slow like a snail,
I race to nowhere, on a whimsical trail.
Emails ping, but I just hit snooze,
In the wake of my tasks, I'm in a nice cruise.

The kitchen timer's my trusted mate,
I set it to cook, but it seals my fate.
I start a new project; wait, is that cheese?
Oh look, a distraction, how easy to please!

I juggle my plans, but oh what a sight,
Like a clown in a circus, it's pure delight.
A dance with futility, oh how I twirl,
With a sprinkle of chaos, let laughter unfurl!

So here I am, stuck in delight,
With glitter and giggles, I'll take flight.
Moments unfold like a roll of fresh tape,
And in their embrace, I just laugh and escape.

Harvesting Hope from the Dust

Underneath the couch, hope grows wild,
Dust bunnies dancing, they're easily riled.
I search for lost dreams like they're Easter eggs,
While munching on cookies, my procrastination begs.

The garden of wishes needs sunshine and care,
But right now, I'm seated without a single scare.
Weed out the worries with laughter and fun,
And maybe, just maybe, I'll get something done!

An empty planner, a canvas so bright,
Ideas like popcorn, pop left and right.
I gather them slowly, like treasure on sand,
Then lose half my harvest – it's all unplanned!

So here's a toast to the dreams slightly bent,
To stumbles and giggles, to time that's well spent.
As I dust off the shelves, I cheer with a grin,
Who knew that the journey was where it begins?

The Narrow Path to Understanding

Wisdom is wandering in shoes too tight,
As I fumble my way through this puzzling plight.
Stumbling on answers like pebbles in shoes,
With laughter as balm, I embrace the blues.

Why am I here? Oh, let's make a bet,
With a riddle or two, it's slightly upset.
Questions abound like confetti in air,
Yet each laugh I share brings me closer to care.

The narrow path twists like spaghetti at noon,
I slide to the left, but the right's a monsoon.
With chuckles and snorts, I dodge all the wrong,
In the comedy of life, I can't help but belong!

So let's skip to the end with a wink and a nod,
Life's a ridiculous and joyful facade.
And though I may wander, I find with a grin,
The things that I seek are where laughter begins.

Tracing Circles in the Sand

I made a plan, it vanished fast,
Like footprints left as waves rolled past.
My goals are like beach balls in flight,
Bouncing around, oh what a sight!

With every step, I lose my way,
Chasing seagulls that laugh and play.
My watch just laughs at the sand I chase,
Time's on a break, it's lost in space.

I draw a map with a stick in hand,
But it leads to nowhere in this sandy land.
The crabs all giggle at my grand plan,
'What's your next move?' they ask with a tan.

But oh, how I love this game on the shore,
Tracing circles—you can't ask for more!
So here's to the joy, the slip and the slide,
In this goofy adventure, I'll take a ride!

Where the Unspoken Lives

In a land where silence gets loud applause,
Whispers of dreams trip over their claws.
We gather our thoughts in a juggling act,
Balancing hopes that come with a pact.

The coffee pot gossips, spills all it knows,
Filling our cups with brewed prose and woes.
Invisible ink writes the tales of our hearts,
But it smudges and fades before the fun starts.

We speak in riddles, a laugh in disguise,
That comes like surprise through half-opened eyes.
Imaginary friends join the dance on the walls,
They roller-skate through, giggle, and fall.

Yet here in the stillness, we figure it out,
In laughter and chaos, we thrash and shout.
Where the unspoken blooms, bright and alive,
Here's where we flourish, and truly arrive!

The Tug of Juxtaposed Dreams

A dream of a castle, a dream of a car,
One wants to fly, and the other—go far.
With each little tug, my mind runs a race,
One pulls at sunshine, the other—deep space.

Picture this circus, where clowns run amok,
In a tangle of wishes, my brain is struck.
The bus or the broomstick, which one do I ride?
Life's just a game, who's keeping score inside?

A jester made of candy and soft-serve ice cream,
Winks at my choices, like "What's your dream scheme?"
I flip-flop on options, just like a fish,
Caught in a bowl, still dreaming my wish.

And in this tug-of-war, I happily grin,
For the mix of my dreams is where I begin.
So bring on the chaos, the fun and the cheer,
In this playful mess, my path becomes clear!

Shadows of Ambition

In a shadowy room where ideas take flight,
A dream dressed in polka dots, ready to bite.
My visions all giggle, they dance on the walls,
Planting their feet in imaginary halls.

Oh, I'll climb that mountain! Or wait—let's just sing,
To the tune of uncertainty, oh what joy it brings!
With flip-flops and bubbles, we plot out our schemes,
In the shadows of laughter, we cling to our dreams.

The ladder is rickety, the steps are absurd,
Yet still I persist, though no one's disturbed.
The light overhead flickers, just like my plan,
Yet out of this chaos, a new laugh began.

So here's to the shadows and all that they do,
They tickle our fancy and give hope its cue.
We'll muddle through moments, they're oddly profound,
In this funny parade, my ambition is found!

Building Bridges to Tomorrow

I'm crafting a bridge with just some string,
Hoping it leads to some grand new bling.
The plans are all scribbled, I can't find the tape,
But who needs instructions? It's all a big cape.

With every wrong nail, the structure sways,
They say I'm a builder in so many ways.
Just like my breakfast, it's all a big mess,
Yet who knew a bridge could wear such a dress?

I ask for a level, they laugh and they scoff,
With a wink and a smile, they all just back off.
I'm building a bridge that might not quite last,
But hey, it's the journey—let's forget the past.

In this silly endeavor, I'm betting it's clear,
The bridge might just lead to a world full of cheer.
And if it should crumble, let's not shed a tear,
I'll just grab my ukulele and bring in some beer.

Quiet Reflections in a Running Stream

I sit by the stream, with a pebble or two,
It's quiet here, just a bird in the blue.
I toss in my thoughts, watch them float on by,
Like my hopes of becoming a famous pie guy.

The water keeps gurgling, like it knows a joke,
While I'm here pondering life in this cloak.
Each ripple conceals my dreams unfulfilled,\nBut I wave at the fish—'You're so well-skilled!'

The moon peeks in, does a cheeky dance,
As I muse on the chances of not taking a chance.
What's life without giggles and floating around?
I'll stick to my stream, where my joy can be found.

With a splash and a laugh, let the worries go free,
In this running stream, there's just me and some tea.
The heart of the moment drifts quietly near,
And suddenly, being absurd feels just right here.

In the Midst of Uncertainty

Here I stand on a cliff, feeling rather bold,
With options galore, but still feeling cold.
Should I jump to the left or carefully sway?
It's a dance of confusion, let's party today!

Maps and compasses all lie upside down,
I wear my own crown, though I'm not sure of a town.
The path is a riddle, yet I chart my own course,
While giggles and snickers keep fueling the force.

Every twist and turn feels like a new game,
Guessing where I'm off to—nothing feels the same.
But in this wild ride, there's a glittering glee,
As I trip on my shoelaces and call it "free spree."

When the road takes a leap, I just take in a breath,
Navigating life's jokes with humor from death.
So here's to the chaos that dances around,
In the midst of the clueless, my joy can be found.

Echoes of an Unheard Call

I'm waiting for answers, they seem so far off,
Like whispers in wind that just giggle and scoff.
I dial up the future, but it goes to voicemail,
And I'm left with my thoughts, sipping cups of "do not fail."

The echoes of dreams bounce around in my mind,
Like a squirrel with acorns, rather unrefined.
I chase these reflections, I chase after light,
But my shadow keeps tripping on sneakers too tight.

Unheard messages ringing, tonight they will stay,
Just fragments and blips in this complex buffet.
I question my choices like socks without mates,
But laughter arises, oh the joy it creates!

So, here in the silence, my heart finds its song,
A tune of confusion where awkward belongs.
With every strange echo, I giggle and grin,
In the chaos of whispers, I find my way in!

In the Half-Formed Horizon

In the middle of nowhere, I stand,
With a map drawn in crayon, quite bland.
Clouds above me are just cotton candy,
Is my life just one big unplanned dandy?

Looking for signs that might not exist,
Every detour feels like a twist.
A squirrel passes by, gives me a wink,
I laugh and wonder, what do I think?

Chasing shadows in bright sunlight,
Searching for meaning, without insight.
A dance party with my lost socks,
In the quest of life, who needs any blocks?

So here I am, stuck in my head,
Living on whims, not much to dread.
I'll ride this wave of absurdity,
Until the day I discover my clarity!

The Quest for Meaning Unfolds

In the search for a clue, I trip on my shoelace,
Falling in laughter, oh what a pace!
My goals fly high like a kite on a spree,
Yet still stuck in my chair—oh, woe is me!

A cup of coffee, spilled on the floor,
Maybe spilled wisdom? I could use more.
With thoughts like confetti that float in the air,
I try to catch meaning—but it just isn't there!

A dance-off with my reflection in glass,
Each move a question, will I ever pass?
As I twirl through the mess, socks clashing in glee,
Wondering if I'm just too lazy to see.

When the sun sets, and the stars come to play,
I laugh at my journey, come what may.
One day I'll find that elusive thing,
But for now, let's dance and joyfully sing!

Yet to Be Written

In a book that's blank, my story awaits,
Plot twists and punchlines behind big gates.
With a feather pen and a bottle of ink,
I scribble my thoughts, with the faintest of links.

Ticklish thoughts dance like leaves in the breeze,
Collecting ideas like fireflies—oh, please!
A character named Gary who can't find the door,
Through walls he bumbles, oh, what's in store?

I shuffle the pages, unsure of my fate,
Each line a giggle, each verse a plate.
Who needs a plot? I'll just wing it today,
Living for laughter, come what may!

The ink spills laughter, the pages get bold,
As my story unfolds, it's comically told.
So here's to the journey, absurd and free,
In this half-written tale, just watch and see!

Echoes of an Unfinished Journey

In a world where I wander, a clown at the fair,
I trip over meanings, float high in the air.
A map made of jelly, it wiggles and shakes,
Where do I go next? Oh, for goodness' sakes!

With echoes of laughter trailing behind,
I search for that gem that's so hard to find.
My life spins like tops in a child's game,
Each spin a question I'm too proud to claim.

A pie in the sky, a rhyme without reason,
Is it summer or winter? Oh, what is the season?
I dance on the edges of dreams and desires,
With flamenco flair, and a sprinkle of fires!

So here's to the echoes that tickle my soul,
On this journey, my friends, we're all on a stroll.
With punchlines aplenty and giggles in store,
In this unfinished journey, who could ask for more?

Threads of Time Yet to Weave

In the loom of life we fumble,
Caught in threads that twist and tumble.
Stitch by stitch, we try to craft,
But most designs end up a draft.

The needle's sharp, we prick our fate,
Knots get tangled, oh what a state!
Patterns fade, the fabric thickens,
Must we always make such quick decisions?

The fabric shop sells dreams anew,
We pick the colors, bright and blue.
But in each patch, a story's hidden,
Of laughter, love, and things unwritten.

So here we stand, with tape and glue,
Fixing holes and buying time too.
Our masterpiece will come to show,
When life decides it's time to sew!

The Pause Before the Leap

Standing at the edge, unsure,
Gazing down, can I endure?
A jump of faith, that's what they say,
But my socks are mismatched today!

Friends shout, "Just go, it's no big deal!"
I laugh, though my nerves spin the wheel.
"If I fall, will I bounce like a ball?"
Or will I pancake? Oh dear, not at all!

Now counting down, with a twist and turn,
For every second, new lessons to learn.
A leap of joy or a flop of shame?
Guess it'll be both—who's keeping the scoregame?

With one big push, I'm ready for fun,
Will I make it? Oh wait, maybe run!
The pause is over, here I go steep,
Into the unknown, take the leap, I peep!

Reflections on a Broken Star

A star fell down, right on my head,
I thought it'd quit, but it just bled.
"Wish upon me!", it gasped in pain,
But all I got was a leaky brain!

In cosmic café, sipping stardust brew,
I ponder dreams that never grew.
The sparkles fade, the night gets long,
Maybe I'm just singing a silly song.

Mirrors shatter, but I'm still here,
Collecting fragments, oh dear, oh dear!
That broken star can't complete its flight,
But I'll dance with shadows under the night.

So here's to the stars that fell from grace,
They bring out the laughter in this odd space.
When life gets dark and feels too bizarre,
Just catch a smile from a broken star!

Unfinished Symphony of the Soul

Instruments here are out of tune,
While the conductor hums a whimsical tune.
The notes fly off in crazy array,
As we all dance in a disheveled ballet.

The piano's keys just want to play,
But someone's missing, gone astray.
With every beat my heart takes flight,
Will I ever find the missing sight?

A clarinet croaks like a toad in delight,
While violins scratch in the moonlight.
It's a jam session in chaos bright,
Yet somehow it feels just right.

So here we are, with smiles and muse,
An unfinished piece, with so much to lose.
When life hits a flat, don't lose your flow,
Just let the laughter in — let it grow!

Fragments of a Unmanifested Self

In the mirror, I see my dreams,
But they giggle and sprout funny memes.
Wandering thoughts on a snack break,
Waiting for life's great pancake.

Plans floating like balloons in the sky,
Some wander off, just too shy.
I take a step, but trip in delight,
The universe just loves a good fright.

My ambitions dance with socks on the floor,
While my ideas shout, "We want more!"
But here I stand, twitching with glee,
Still buffering as far as I see.

So here's to the chaos, the awkward and strange,
To waking up and then rearranging.
I laugh with my shadows, they tickle my soul,
Waiting for a plan that's entirely whole.

The Undiscovered Road

Traveling down a road unknown,
Where the map's just food stains and a half-eaten scone.
Every corner turned is a surprise or a snack,
In this lifey ride, there's never a lack.

I met a cactus who sang off-key,
It was the highlight of my bizarre spree.
With two left feet and a pancake on hand,
I pirouette past dreams I can't quite understand.

A frog in a tutu offers me a leap,
"Join us!" they croak, "We're a merry sheep!"
But I tripped over thoughts that led me astray,
Dodging ideas that dance and play.

Yet still onward I stroll, with a smile so wide,
Collecting oddities along for the ride.
The road's still unfolding, new sights every day,
And laughter, dear friends, paves the way.

Waiting for the Green Light

Life's a stoplight that plays with my head,
One moment I'm zipping, the next I'm dead.
With feet on the brakes I sip my cold drink,
While my ambitions just sit and blink.

The red now turns yellow, a cautious delight,
I wiggle and giggle, oh what a sight!
Cars honk like they're in a horn symphony,
As I question my life like a botched recipe.

I see folks zoom past, with checkered flags to claim,
While I'm stuck here playing a waiting game.
But hey, there's a bird with a sparkle in eye,
Teaching me patience, oh me, oh my!

So here I shall wait, with a grin on my face,
For soon I shall thrive, at my own goofy pace.
Green light, oh please, don't be so shy,
I'm ready to race under this big, bright sky.

Chasing Shadows of Intent

I chase shadows that tease and run,
In this game of life, we're never done.
They wiggle and jiggle, like jello on a plate,
And I'm left in stitches, can't seem to relate.

My plans skip rope like they're in a show,
The clearer my thoughts, the faster they go.
With a rubber band heart and a vest full of dreams,
I tackle each day with snickers and beams.

Intentions play tag with a mischievous grin,
I laugh as I stumble, no need to fit in.
With shadows that flicker and dance in delight,
I'm just here for giggles, zany and bright.

So I'll keep on twirling, with dreams in my hand,
Chasing those shadows, it's all unplanned.
For who needs a map when the laughter's so loud?
In the carnival of life, I'll twirl with the crowd.

The Quest for Unseen Horizons

In my quest to find the light,
A compass spins, it feels just right.
With every step, I trip and fall,
Is there a guide, or none at all?

Maps are drawn in crayon hues,
A treasure's marked, but which to choose?
Pirates laugh, I'm lost at sea,
But wait, is that a squirrel I see?

I ponder life beneath the stars,
While counting all the silly cars.
Their tires squeak, they seem to tease,
The answer's here, just hang with ease!

The humor in this grand charade,
We tickle fate, no need for shade.
In every blunder, wisdom's found,
With laughter's echo all around.

In Search of Meaning

I wandered through a coffee shop,
Searching deep for a wisdom drop.
The barista winked, 'A latte's key!'
But it's just caffeine, or could it be?

Notes of wisdom line the walls,
"Do not feed squirrels" – who recalls?
Yet here I sit, not sure of why,
Maybe my brain's too big to fly?

Philosophers dance in my head,
With half-baked thoughts, I might be dead.
They bicker on the nature of bread,
As I just want to find my bed!

But wait! A thought begins to bloom,
Perhaps I'm meant to sit and fume.
For in this chaos, laughs abound,
The meaning's lost, but joy is found!

Whispers of the Waiting Heart

My heart whispers like a shy cat,
It ponders life while wearing a hat.
"Where's the meaning?" it softly quips,
While I twirl round in my own scripts.

Tick-tock goes the clock on the wall,
I wait for answers, hear them call.
But mostly, I just hear my snack,
Popcorn crunching — oh, what a knack!

As I gaze out at the setting sun,
The universe just laughs for fun.
"Chase the light!" a wise voice said,
But I'm still busy staring at bread!

Yet amidst this dance of time and fate,
The heart waits on, it's never late.
With gentle giggles and silly tunes,
It learns to hum beneath the moons.

Dreams in the Balance

On a tightrope strung with silly strings,
I juggle dreams and other things.
A rubber chicken flies on by,
Just as I reach for that pie in the sky!

Balancing life with one shoe on,
With each misstep, I start to yawn.
The world seems like a wobbly dance,
In every stumble, there's a chance!

I chase success with a grin so wide,
But my pizza slice cannot hide.
It twirls around like a merry sprite,
As I ponder wrongs and rights!

Yet laughter lends a softer hand,
In dreams that waver, but still stand.
So I'll embrace this clumsy ride,
With humor's spark, my heart's my guide.

The Mystery of Uncharted Waters

I sailed a boat made of toast,
In waters thick with surprise most.
With jellyfish that wore a tie,
And fish that sang a lullaby.

I asked the waves, 'What's my fate?'
They whispered back, 'Just wait, just wait!'
A sea of maps with routes untraced,
And mermaids giggling, still displaced.

The compass spun with glee and fright,
As I rode waves of sheer delight.
Each splash was laughter, a sunny gig,
In sea of dreams, I danced a jig.

So here I float, in bread I trust,
As fortune smiles, and sails combust.
From uncharted depths I'll soon emerge,
In goofy dreams, I will submerge.

Building Bridges in the Fog

I tried to build a bridge from dreams,
With popsicle sticks and silly schemes.
Fog rolled in like a thick gray soup,
While friendly birds formed quite a troupe.

With every plank a laugh erupted,
As squirrels watched on, completely disrupted.
I thought I'd cross but took a dip,
Instead, became the bridge's trip!

The fog now giggled, thick and round,
As I flailed about, lost and bound.
Yet through the haze, a rooster crowed,
And suddenly, all my fears erode.

So here I stand, a builder bold,
With laughter's warmth against the cold.
In that mist, I found my cheer,
Bridges formed from giggles, dear.

Flickers of a Dream Yet to Bloom

In a garden where the daisies dance,
I planted seeds with a hopeful glance.
Yet all that sprouted were socks and fluff,
As bumblebees critiqued my stuff.

With every flicker, a wish took flight,
In a pot that once held pasta bright.
Hoping for roses, I got a shoe,
And butterflies wearing hats of blue.

"Oh dear," I mused, scratching my head,
"Perhaps this garden's a dream misled?"
Yet out from dirt, a giggle arose,
A flower with a face and a funny prose.

So here I sit, in my quirky glade,
With blooms of humor that never fade.
For laughter's seeds planted within,
Shall always sprout, a joyful grin.

Amidst the Unanswered Questions

I pondered life like a spinning top,
Why does my shoe disappear, then plop?
In mysteries wrapped in curious bits,
Like socks that vanish, the truth that splits.

As I questioned the stars and their grand parade,
A cat appeared, in shades of jade.
"Why are we here?" I boldly asked,
He yawned, then napped, no answers unmasked.

With every riddle, a giggle rang,
As worms danced along and the frogs sang.
"Just enjoy the ride, don't fret too much,"
Said a wise old owl with a silly touch.

So here I stand, amidst whims and whims,
In life's vast stage, where hope swims.
With jokes and laughter, I'll find my way,
Through unanswered questions, I'll laugh and play.

Shadows of a Work in Progress

In the quiet of night, I ponder my fate,
Coffee in hand, I'm never too late.
Ideas dance wildly, like squirrels at play,
But focus escapes me, just one more delay.

Tasks pile up higher, a colorful stack,
I swear I'll get to it, just hold the snack.
Patterns emerge, like socks from the wash,
But for now, I'm just free-wheeling this nosh.

Each doodle a dream, a sketch of the grand,
Yet somehow my scribbles go right off the hand.
But laughter does find me, in moments of dread,
As I trip on my vision, and fall on my head.

So here I remain, in this whimsical state,
Crafting a future that just has to wait.
With a wink and a nod, I embrace the absurd,
In this game of confusion, my thoughts are unstirred.

Whispers of Tomorrow's Promise

In the garden of thought, seeds flutter about,
Like butterflies lost, they complain and they shout.
The plans I have made, they flutter away,
And here I am sitting—was that yesterday?

Cartwheeling dreams on a merry-go-round,
Finding my footing on loose, shaky ground.
Magic is lazy when time's on the prowl,
Crafting a show, but I'm lost in the towel.

Chasing great visions that sparkle and shine,
But tripping on shoe laces, oh, isn't it fine?
I'll think about work as I snack on some pie,
But first, let me ponder the clouds in the sky.

So whisper to me, of the futures ahead,
Where dancing with purpose keeps me out of bed.
For now, I will giggle, a bubble of hope,
A playful delight as I wriggle and grope.

Beyond the Edge of Clarity

Nudging the fog, a vision appears,
A jester with crowns thinks he runs on the gears.
Painted with patience, each step is a jest,
As I play with ideas, with whimsical zest.

A compass that spins, amid chuckles and cheers,
Guides me through mazes of colorful fears.
Maps form and dissolve like ice cream on breath,
A tasty endeavor, flirting with death.

With sketches of rabbits that float on a line,
And umbrellas that dance like they're feeling quite fine.
I giggle at dreams that refuse to be true,
Meanwhile, I sip on my laughably brew.

So here's to the chaos that makes up our hearts,
Where laughter eludes, but confusion imparts.
Beyond all the plans, and the meticulous games,
The humor of life turns purpose to flames.

Chasing the Flickering Flame

With a lollipop in hand, I chase after spark,
A light that's elusive, it's bold and it's dark.
Where wisdom tumbles like marbles in play,
And clarity hides, just around the next sway.

I chase after whispers of flickering thoughts,
Wielding some humor, like bags full of knots.
Peering through shadows, I leap with a grin,
As sparks turn to kites, and my laughter logs in.

Juggling my worries, I fall on my face,
Yet giggles erupt in this curious place.
With fingers a-fumble, I scramble the truth,
Yet joy paints my canvas, recalling my youth.

So watch as I dart like a comet set free,
Chasing the flickers, my mind's jubilee.
For life's just a dance, a spark in the night,
Where laughter ignites and dreams take own flight.

When the Compass Spins

Lost in the woods, no map in sight,
The compass spins, it's quite a sight.
It points to dinner, with starry flair,
I guess I'll just plan a picnic there.

A squirrel laughs, it knows the way,
But I can't seem to chase it away.
The North Star winked, I swear it spoke,
'Just follow your nose, and you'll find hope!'

My GPS plays hide and seek,
It claims it's strong, but feels quite weak.
It updates slow, like turtle's pace,
I'll ask the trees, they know this place.

With every turn, the laughter grows,
Maybe I'll just follow my toes.
The compass spins, and so does my head,
I'll wander forever, or just go to bed.

Waiting for the Signal

Staring at my phone, it's gone all dark,
I'd give it a poke, but it's lost its spark.
The Wi-Fi's weak, it left the room,
I guess I'll just wait for the signal's bloom.

In the café, I sip my tea,
Watching people, as they flee.
My phone's a ninja, hiding away,
Playing too hard, it won't come out to play.

Someone's yelling, "It's back online!"
But I'm still stuck in this endless line.
I check my coat, my nose, my jeans,
No signal found in these old seams!

So I wave goodbye to my plan of fun,
Guess I'll just chat with my bread 'til I'm done.
'Twas a date with tech, now it's canceled, alas!
When in doubt, at least there's this muffin to pass.

Navigating the In-Between

In the land of maybe, I roam free,
Between what is and what might be.
Maps are confusing, directions unclear,
I'm just looking for snacks, my dear!

Lost in thought, I take a stand,
"Oh look, a donut! Isn't life grand?"
I trip on wishes, fall into dreams,
Reality's busting at the seams.

Between the couch and distant shore,
I scavenge crumbs from the floor.
Happiness levels? Believe you me,
They rise when marshmallows are in my tea.

Navigating paths of chocolate delight,
I'll ponder deep into the night,
For in-betweens are where I play,
With laughter ringing and snacks on display.

Searching for Threads of Gold

In a pile of laundry, I dig with care,
Hoping to find treasures hiding there.
Socks go missing, but what's the score?
I've struck sequins, not diamonds nor more!

A breadcrumb trail of oddities found,
Like mismatched buttons from a lost surround.
With every peek, a chuckle unfolds,
Who knew laundry could spin tales so bold?

Car keys, loose change, and a toy from '92,
This washing machine's been busy, who knew?
As I rumble through this state of bliss,
For the thrill of the hunt, nothing's amiss!

Threads of gold? Just a myth they say,
But here in my basket, I'll laugh and play.
In every wrinkle and odd little fold,
I'm rich in stories, more precious than gold.

Unseen Wind Beneath Our Wings

We float on clouds of endless thought,
But where's the breeze we truly sought?
With vacant eyes and hopeful grin,
We wonder where this flight begins.

The birds above just laugh and sing,
As we contemplate our silly thing.
To soar or nap? What's our best plan?
The choice is tough for this tired man.

A gust arrives, the world does spin,
Did we remember to pack a grin?
With every flap, our hearts take flight,
Through fluffy dreams and sheer delight.

So here we glide, not quite sure why,
Chasing laughter in the sky.
With unseen wind beneath our wings,
Life's a game of guessing things.

Dreams Dibbling in Syllables

Words dance like ants across the page,
In caps and curls, they start to stage.
But wait, is this a dream or what?
A jumbled mess in a coffee cup!

Oh scribble here, and doodle there,
My brain's a carnival, I swear!
In search of rhyme, I trip and fall,
Spinning pots and pans, oh, how they call!

Each line a circus, bizarre and bright,
With clowns emerging from the light.
A juggler's fate, it's a twisty show,
In every word, my thoughts will flow.

So join the fun, come lend an ear,
Laugh at the chaos brought so near.
The dreams are dibbling, can't you see?
In silliness, we find the key!

Peeking Through the Veil

A curtain twitch, a monkey's glance,
What lies beyond in this odd dance?
Do we find wisdom, laughs, or fear?
Or simply leftovers from last year?

With eyes wide shut, we poke and pry,
In search of magic or a pie.
The veil hangs low, whispering tales,
Of dreams that float like silly snails.

"Why wait for tomorrows that may never come?"
Said the wise tortoise, while chewing gum.
So let's peek through, not stand in line,
Who knew procrastination's divine?

Behind each fold, a riddle sways,
In giggles and grumbles, we spend our days.
So join the fun, it's really no hassle,
Peeking through veils leads to a castle!

Whispers of the Procrastinating Heart

In the quiet nook of a lazy day,
My dreams for tomorrow begin to sway.
With every tick of the clock's embrace,
My heart whispers, 'Let's slow the race!'

"To do or not to do?" it sighs,
As plans turn fuzzy with blinking eyes.
"Perhaps I'll nap just one more hour,
Or binge on snacks—oh, that's real power!"

Outside, the world buzzes with haste,
Yet in my mind, there's no need to race.
With lazy skips, the moments depart,
Amusing dances of a carefree heart.

So let it whisper, let it charm,
Each second stretched, like a wooly arm.
For in this bliss of winding play,
We'll find ourselves, but not today!

Echoes of a Silent Muse

Whispers bounce off empty walls,
Ideas like lost socks in the halls.
Chasing the muse on a pogo stick,
She just laughs, says, "Take your pick!"

Coffee cups stacked like a tower,
Trying to summon creative power.
But the clock ticks loud, mocking my quest,
Silly thoughts at their uninvited best!

Fridges filled with half-eaten snacks,
Inspiration hides, laughing at my tracks.
I scribble notes that make no sense,
Like a penguin trying to climb a fence!

So here I sit, in this mess profound,
With jumbled words that spin around.
Maybe the muse is just stuck in a loop,
Or perhaps she's just busy with the soup!

Harvesting Clarity from Fog

The morning mist is thick and gray,
As I trip on plants that want to play.
I've brought my basket for insights clear,
But all I find is a lost raccoon near!

Foggy thoughts and tangled vines,
The universe says, "Read between the lines!"
I squint at clouds that refuse to budge,
Friendly reminders of a caffeinated grudge.

Where's the clarity in this dense haze?
I chase a thought that quickly decays.
Like trying to catch a rapidly moving fish,
Turns out my plan was just a wobbly wish!

Then a light dawns, it's just me in a quest,
Reaping nonsense, yeah, that's the best!
I laugh at the fog, though it tugs at my brain,
Embracing confusion like a silly game!

The Unfolding Map

I found a map, all crumpled and torn,
Promised adventures, filled with scorn.
But each line just leads to a snack,
Guess all roads here lead to the fridge pack!

Circles and arrows that twist and loop,
Like my thoughts when I'm stuck in a groop.
"X" marks the spot, or so it was said,
I dig up chips instead of treasure or bread!

I wander the pages, searching for clues,
Mind says, "Focus!" but I just snooze.
Maybe the path is right under my nose,
Just me, a sandwich, and a daydream dose!

So I fold the map, give it a sigh,
Who needs a plan? Let's just improvise!
With laughter and snacks, let's set forth in glee,
For the best destination is wherever I be!

Unraveled Threads of Existence

I tug at the strings of time and fate,
With yarn that's tangled and feeling great.
Knots that giggle when I pull too hard,
Like a cat playing with a deck of cards!

Life's a sweater, frayed at the seam,
Each day a stitch, or so I dream.
But as I unravel and yarn starts to flee,
I find silly patterns in the chaos spree.

An octopus wearing a funny hat,
Dancing through the threads, imagine that!
While reality whispers, "Keep it together,"
I sing with the yarn, like light as a feather!

So here I sit, with threads that collide,
Dancing with chaos, I won't run and hide.
In the mix of confusion, I'll craft a delight,
For even lost stitches can shine oh so bright!

Echoes of Half-Realized Dreams

In a haze of hope, I stand tall,
Chasing rainbows that often fall.
Each laugh echoes, a silly jest,
As I wander through a puzzling quest.

With a coffee cup that's half-filled still,
I ponder deep on a mundane thrill.
Maybe I'll dance on a wobbly chair,
Or debate with a cat about life's fair share.

Fuzzy plans like cotton candy,
Sweet and sticky, yet never handy.
I chase the clock, but it's on a break,
Ticking slow with every mistake.

Dreams float by like balloons in flight,
When farts break silence, it feels so right.
I'll drop my map, let my heart steer,
In this quirky ride, there's nothing to fear.

Unfinished Compass

I've got a compass, it spins a lot,
Directionless in a spot I forgot.
It points to snack shops and ice cream stores,
Ignoring the trails that lead to the shores.

With a map that looks more like a doodle,
I find my way through a strange caboodle.
Each x marks the spot of forgotten fun,
While I trip over roots, I laugh, and run.

If I find North, should I keep it? Nah,
Who needs directions when there's s'mores at the bar?
With breadcrumbs trailing snacks I adore,
I follow the crumbs to adventure galore.

Wobbling through life, I'll take the scenic route,
Puns in every corner, oh what a hoot!
The compass laughs, it's clearly a tease,
Drawing me to places that never quite please.

Threads of Tomorrow Unspooled

With yarn in hand, I weave what's bright,
Yet tangled up in my own delight.
A scarf for a squirrel? Perhaps an owl!
I'll knit a hat for a very confused fowl.

The future's fibers fray and bend,
Patterns emerge, but they rarely blend.
I trip on yarn, a colorful mess,
Creating chaos, but feeling no stress.

A tapestry of dreams, but what's the style?
It looks like confetti, yet makes me smile.
Each stitch a giggle, a jab at the norm,
My needles scratching out a joyful swarm.

In the land of unspooled, wild and free,
A raccoon sits, stylishly sipping tea.
To craft is to laugh, and the fun won't stop,
Until I run out of thread—oh, flop!

Navigating through Clouded Paths

With fog in my eyes, I make my way,
Stumbling on clouds, oh what a day!
Every turn hides a chuckle or two,
Maybe I'll meet a dancing kangaroo.

Lost in the mist, but found in the fun,
I chase after giggles as they take off and run.
The sun appears just to throw shade,
I laugh at the shadows it's carelessly made.

A signpost whispers, "Go anywhere near,"
So I stroll to the left, oh dear, oh dear!
Navigating nonsense, with a cheeky grin,
Who knew this journey's a carnival spin?

Through clouded paths where laughter reigns,
Life unfolds its curious chains.
Join in the fun, don't mind the flares,
With silliness thriving, there's joy everywhere.

The Calm in the Chaos

Amid the buzz, I sip my tea,
Planning world change, or maybe just me.
A cat strolls by, with the day so bright,
Guess it's a good time to have a bite.

The crowd rushes, all in a spin,
I tie my shoes and I'm ready to win.
With snacks in hand and thoughts in tow,
I'm the zen master of tipsy flow.

Birds tweet loudly, they're checking their vibe,
While I ponder why I can't do the jive.
Maybe tomorrow I'll dance with flair,
But first, let's see what's beyond my chair.

In chaos, I find my little delight,
A snack, a laugh, oh, that feels just right.
Life's a circus, come take a seat,
Join in the fun, let's make it sweet!

Sketches of a Future Untold

I draw a line, it squiggles and twirls,
Each line is lost in a world of swirls.
I hope to find what lies ahead,
But all I get is doodles instead.

A rocket ship, too tall to fly,
With googly eyes that seem to cry.
My future self just gave a wink,
Then spilled some paint, now what do you think?

Half of my plans come out like art,
The other half? Just a funny part.
I sketch a dream, then watch it fall,
Was that my future? Not at all!

But in the mess, there's laughter loud,
And somehow it feels like I'm quite proud.
So here's to plans that twist and bend,
A future so bright, it needs no mend!

The Art in Anticipation

In every wait, I paint a scene,
Of cupcakes, cats, and a coffee bean.
I twirl my brush with a playful zest,
Anticipation's art is the very best.

Brush strokes fly like butterflies,
Each color chosen brings surprise.
Will tomorrow bring a funny dance?
Or just a nap, a sleepy glance?

I frame my thoughts on the empty wall,
Decorate chaos, ignore the call.
Waiting's a canvas, I fill with cheer,
Let's make each moment a party here!

So let's embrace the thrilling wait,
With funny tales, oh, just contemplate.
Each tick-tock could spin a tale,
In the art of life, we'll never fail!

The Stillness Before the Dawn

The clock ticks slow, and so do I,
A sleepy grin, beneath the sky.
In this quiet, dreams start to sway,
What kind of funny games will play?

The stars blink down, they know my plight,
Will breakfast be eggs or a snack of light?
In stillness, I wonder, then laugh aloud,
You never know what makes you proud.

Each second stretches, like a rubber band,
Do I play it cool or make a stand?
Maybe I'll dance like no one's there,
If morning yawns, I'll just be fair.

So here I lay, in sleepy grace,
As dawn creeps in at its own pace.
With chuckles and quirks, the day unfurls,
In the stillness before the whirls!

www.ingramcontent.com/pod-product-compliance
Lightning Source LLC
Chambersburg PA
CBHW072120070526
44585CB00016B/1510